Beginning Fiddle Duets

for two violins

Book One

written and arranged by Myanna Harvey

CHP303

©2016 by C. Harvey Publications All Rights Reserved.

www.charveypublications.com - print books
www.learnstrings.com - PDF downloadable books
www.harveystringarrangements.com - chamber music

Beginning Fiddle Duets for Two Violins

Written and arranged by Myanna Harvey

Table of Contents

Title	Page
1. Cripple Creek	2
2. Bingo	4
3. Drill Ye Tarriers	5
4. Old Joe Clark	6
5. Erie Canal	8
6. Arkansas Traveler	10
7. I Ride an Old Paint	11
8. Battle Cry of Freedom	12
9. Goober Peas	14
10. Aiken Drum	16
11. Sailor's Jig	18
12. The Muffin Man	20
13. Oh Susannah	22
14. Yankee Doodle	24
15. The Horse and the Flea	26
16. Piper's Jig	28
17. Camptown Races	30
18. Kentucky Lullaby	32

©2016 by C. Harvey Publications All Rights Reserved.

Beginning Fiddle Duets for Two Violins

Cripple Creek

Trad., arr. Myanna Harvey

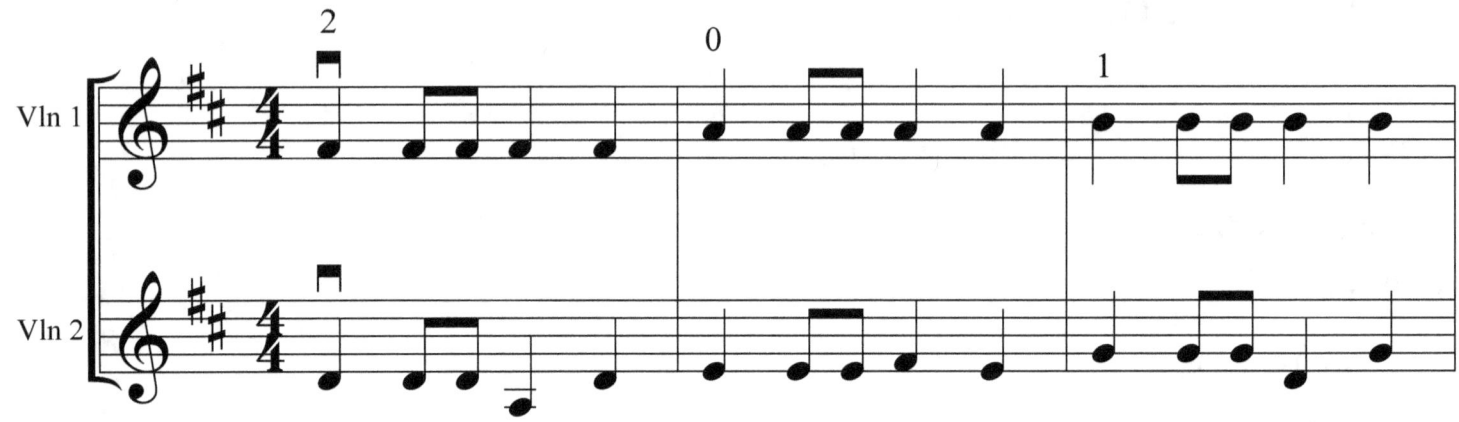

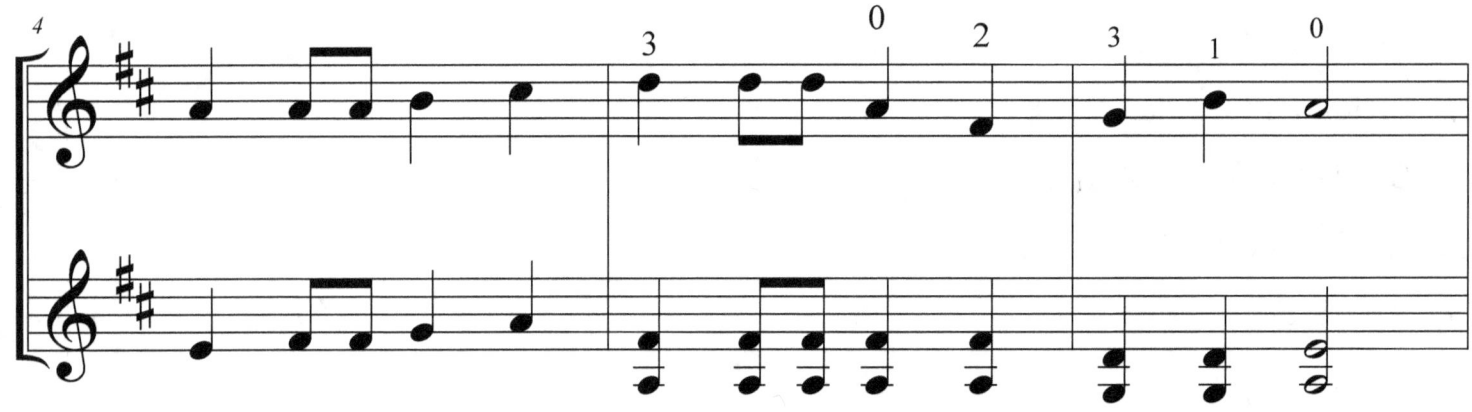

©2016 C. Harvey Publications All Rights Reserved.

Beginning Fiddle Duets for Two Violins

©2016 C. Harvey Publications All Rights Reserved.

Bingo

Trad., arr. Myanna Harvey

Drill Ye Tarriers

Trad., arr. Myanna Harvey

©2016 C. Harvey Publications All Rights Reserved.

Old Joe Clark

Trad., arr. Myanna Harvey

©2016 C. Harvey Publications All Rights Reserved.

Beginning Fiddle Duets for Two Violins

Erie Canal

Trad., arr. Myanna Harvey

©2016 C. Harvey Publications All Rights Reserved.

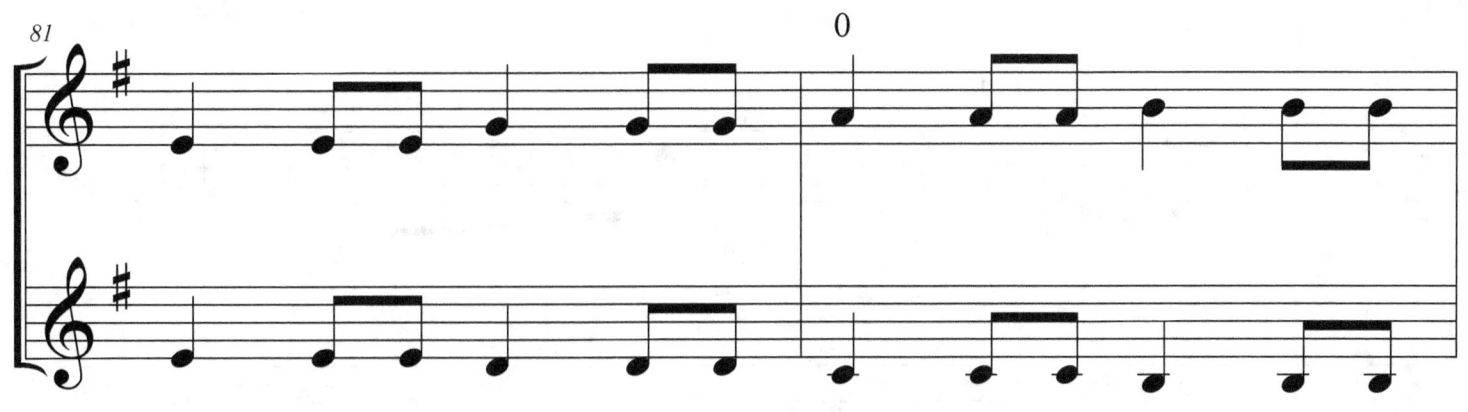

Arkansas Traveler

Trad., arr. Myanna Harvey

I Ride an Old Paint

Trad., arr. Myanna Harvey

Battle Cry of Freedom

Trad., arr. Myanna Harvey

©2016 C. Harvey Publications All Rights Reserved.

Goober Peas

Trad., arr. Myanna Harvey

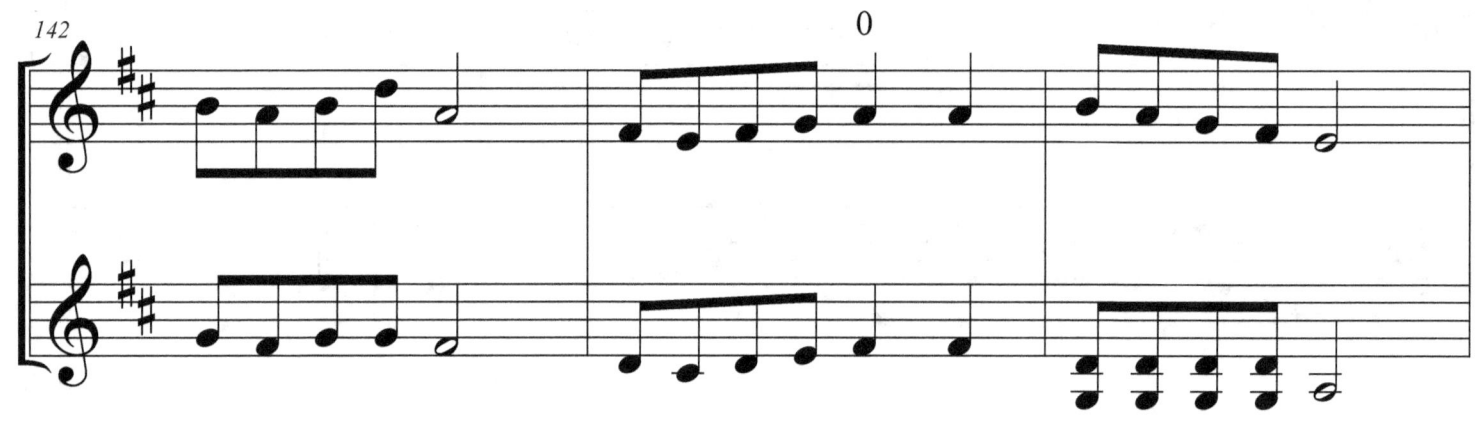

©2016 C. Harvey Publications All Rights Reserved.

Beginning Fiddle Duets for Two Violins, Book One

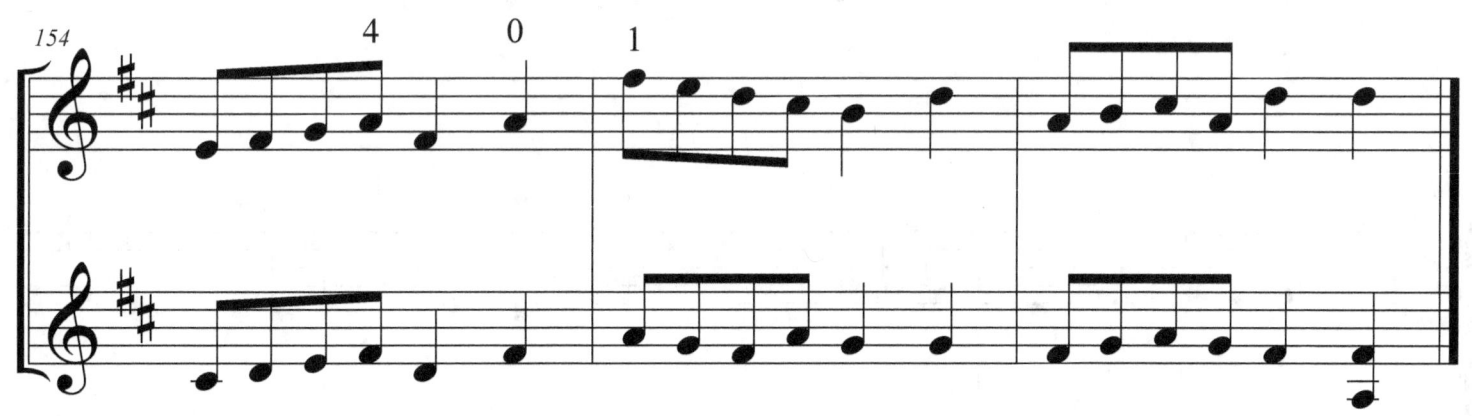

©2016 C. Harvey Publications All Rights Reserved.

Aiken Drum

Trad., arr. Myanna Harvey

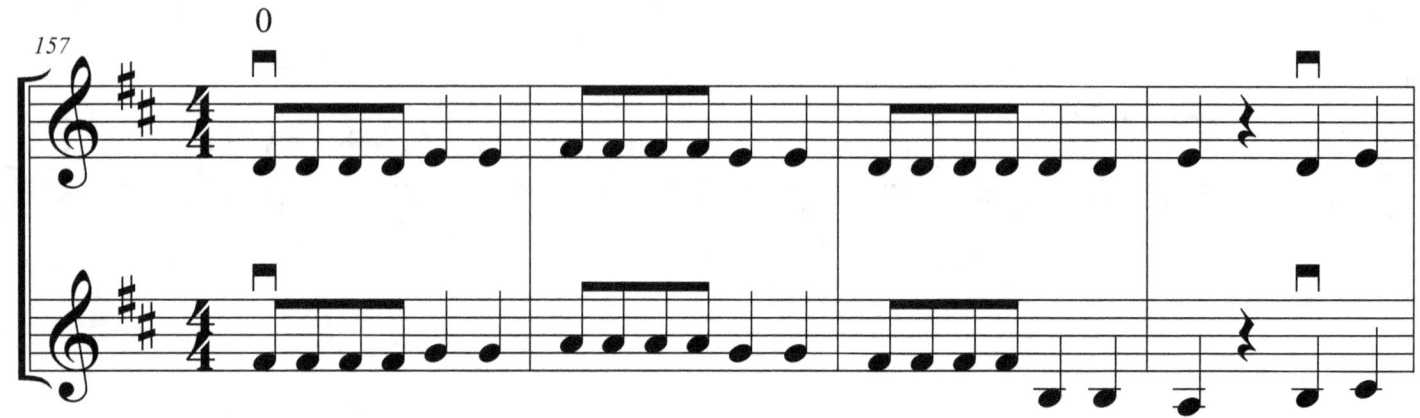
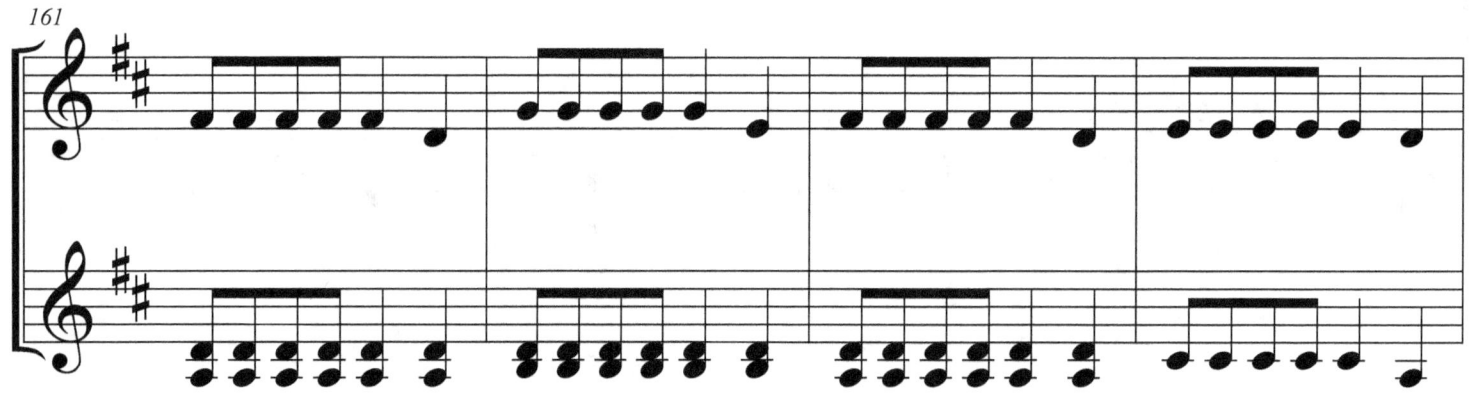
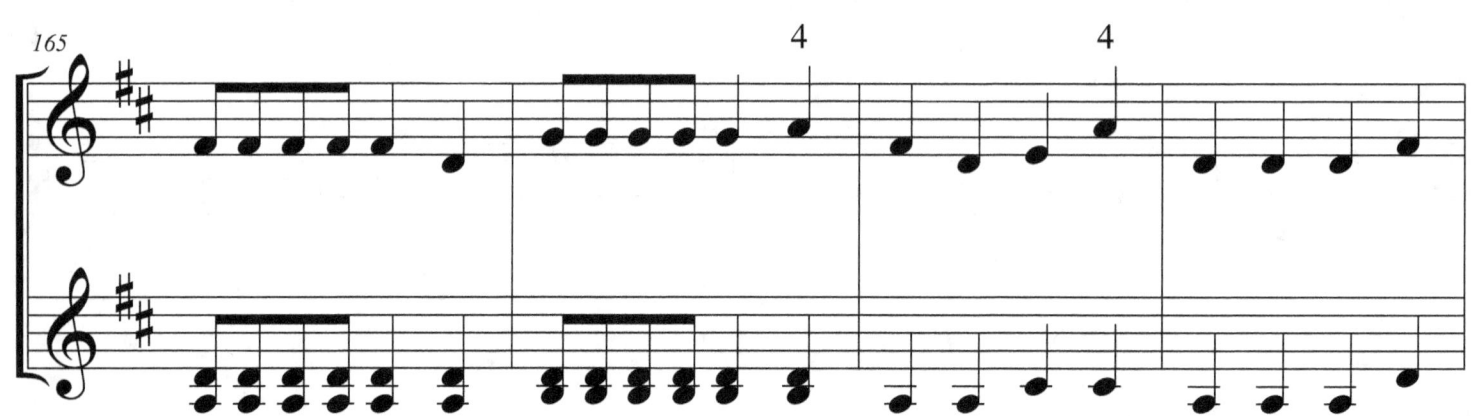

©2016 C. Harvey Publications All Rights Reserved.

Beginning Fiddle Duets for Two Violins, Book One

Sailor's Jig

Myanna Harvey

©2016 C. Harvey Publications All Rights Reserved.

The Muffin Man

Trad., arr. Myanna Harvey

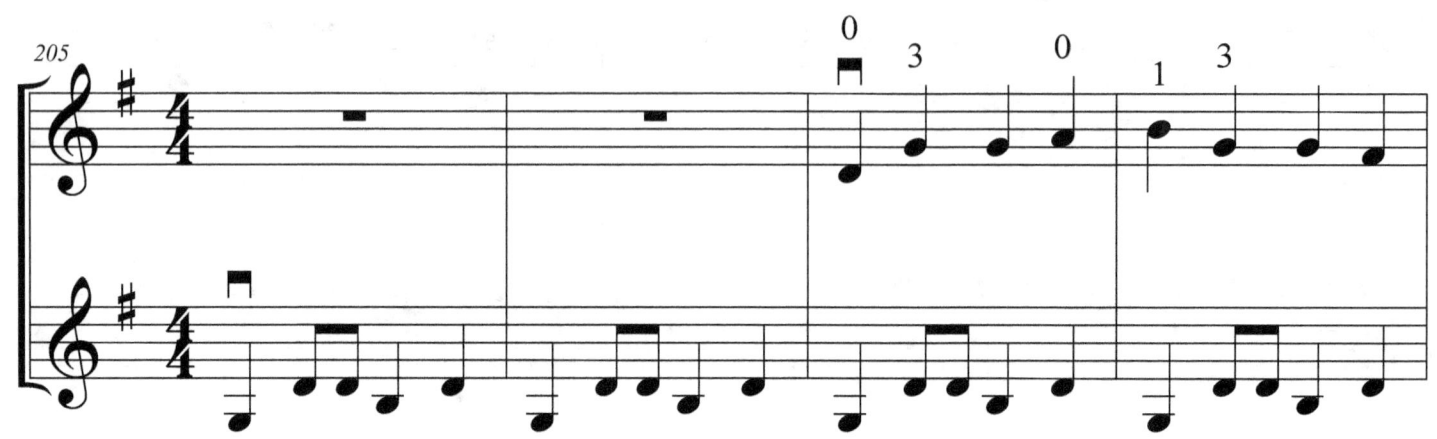

Beginning Fiddle Duets for Two Violins, Book One

Oh Susannah

Foster, arr. Myanna Harvey

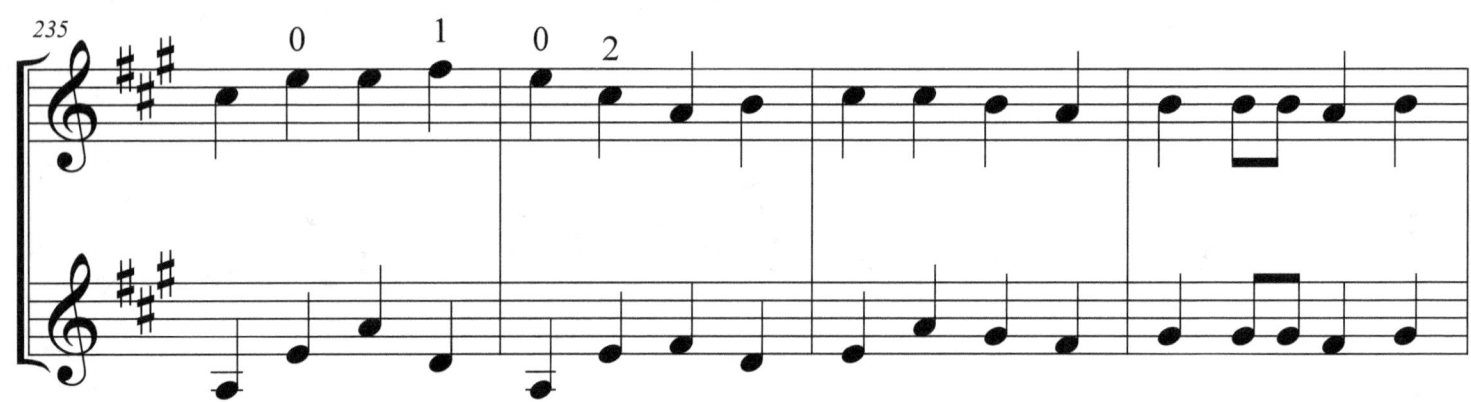
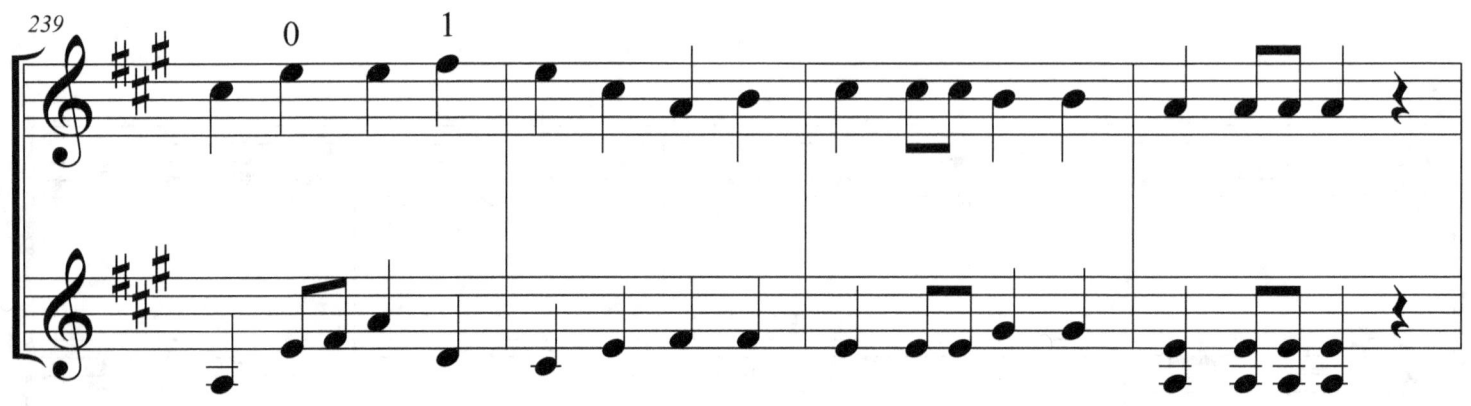

©2016 C. Harvey Publications All Rights Reserved.

Beginning Fiddle Duets for Two Violins, Book One

©2016 C. Harvey Publications All Rights Reserved.

Yankee Doodle

Trad., arr. Myanna Harvey

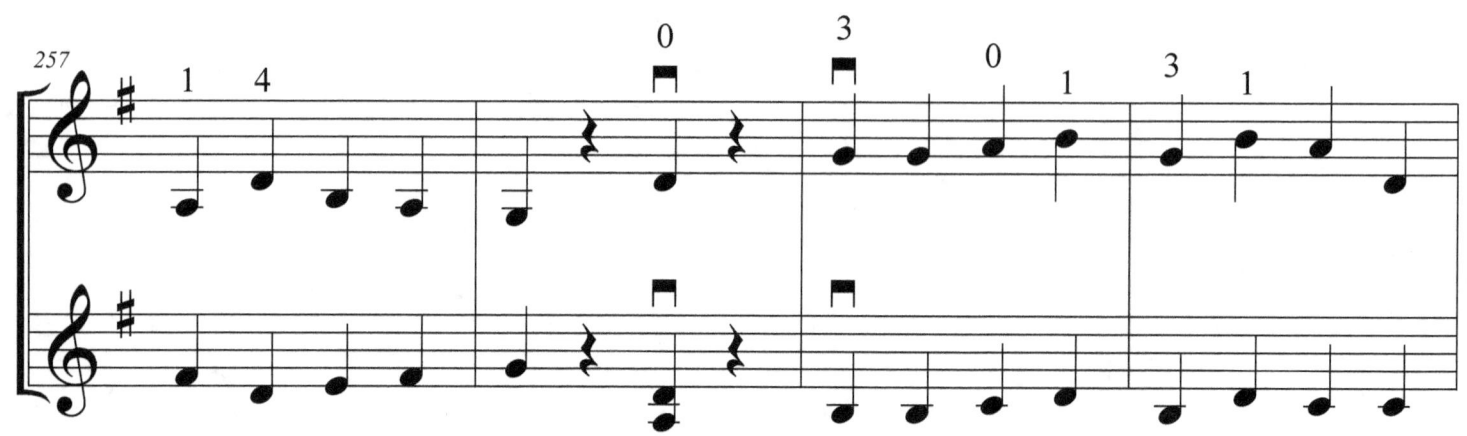

©2016 C. Harvey Publications All Rights Reserved.

Beginning Fiddle Duets for Two Violins, Book One

The Horse and the Flea

Trad., arr. Myanna Harvey

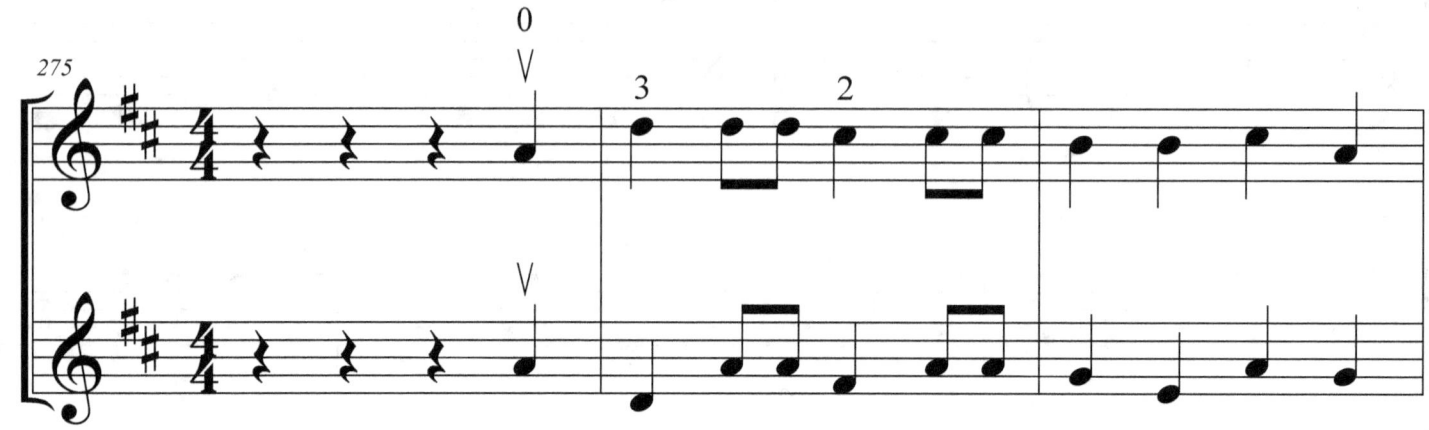

©2016 C. Harvey Publications All Rights Reserved.

Beginning Fiddle Duets for Two Violins, Book One

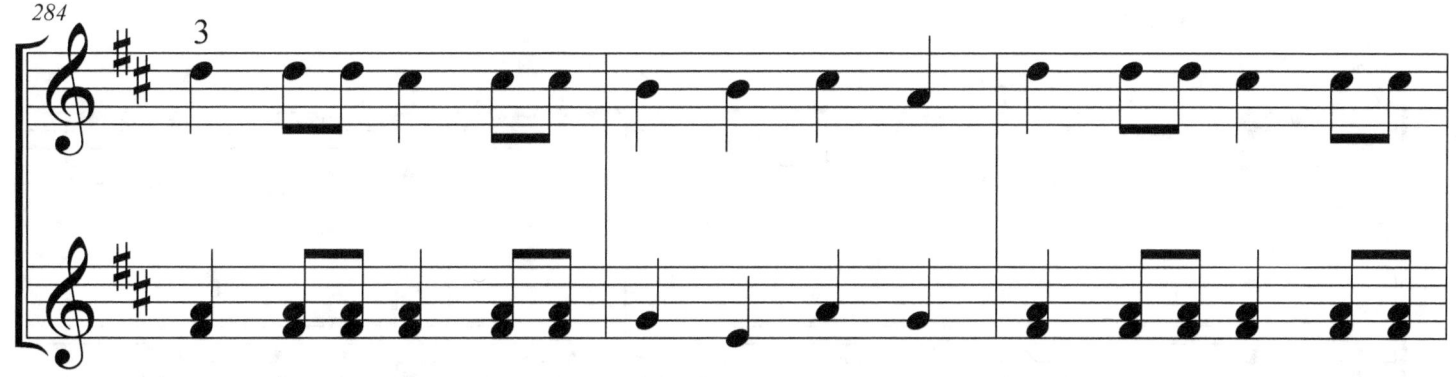

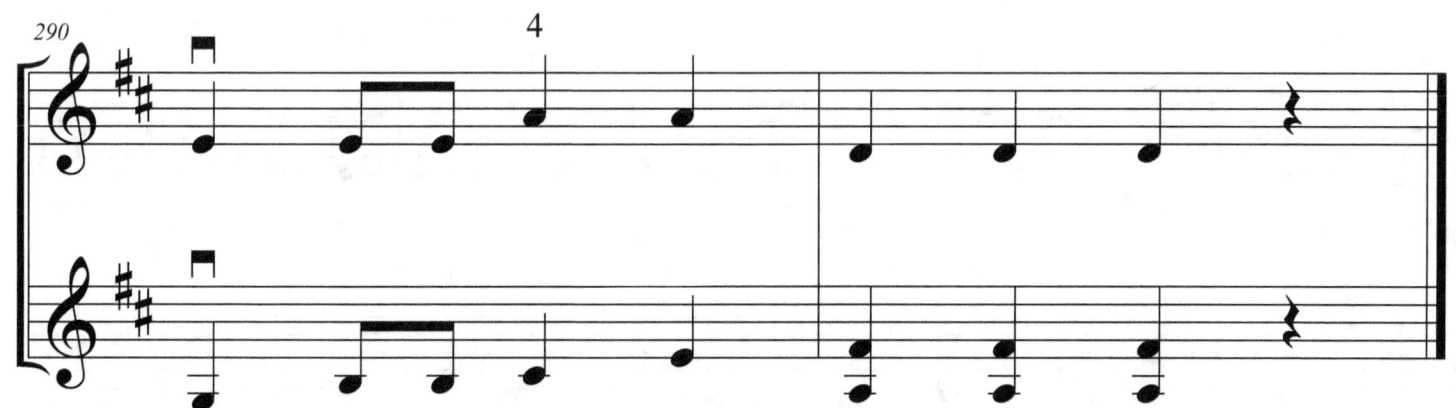

Piper's Jig

Myanna Harvey

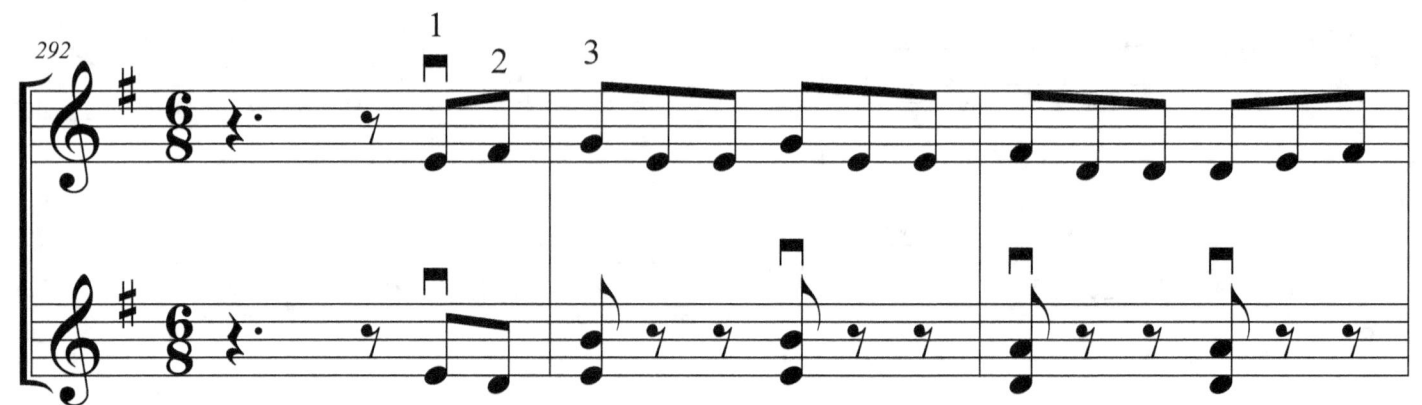
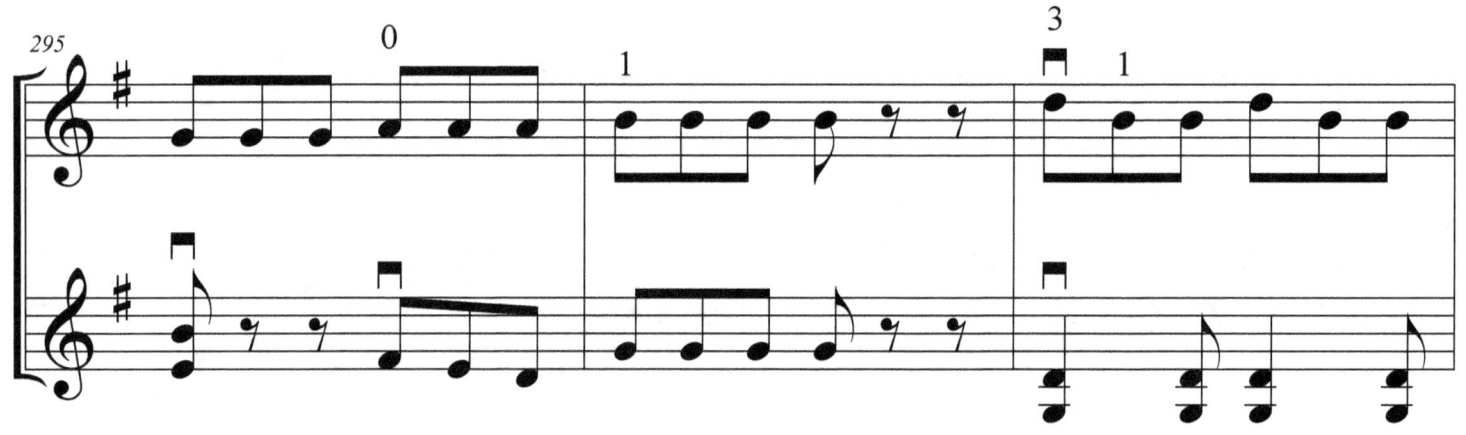
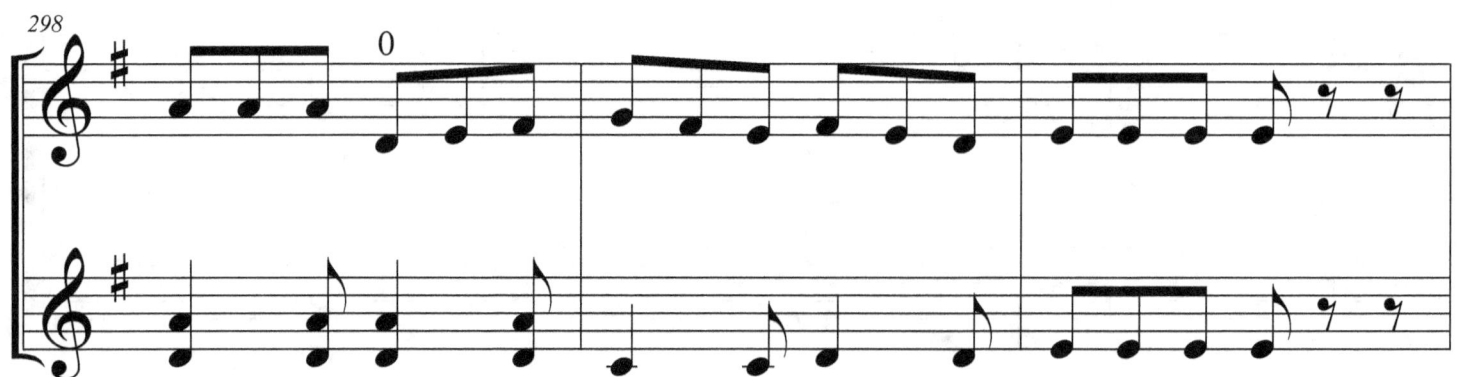

©2016 C. Harvey Publications All Rights Reserved.

Beginning Fiddle Duets for Two Violins, Book One

Camptown Races

Foster., arr. Myanna Harvey

Beginning Fiddle Duets for Two Violins, Book One

Kentucky Lullaby

Trad., arr. Myanna Harvey

Beginning Fiddle Duets for Two Violins, Book One

available from **www.charveypublications.com**: CHP263

Flying Fiddle Duets for Two Violins, Book One

John Ryan's Polka

Trad., arr. Myanna Harvey

©2015 C. Harvey Publications. All Rights Reserved.

www.ingramcontent.com/pod-product-compliance
Lightning Source LLC
Chambersburg PA
CBHW051427070526
44584CB00023B/3618